GOLD RUSH

Alan Trussell-Cullen

NELSON
A Cengage Company

Australia • Brazil • Japan • Korea • Mexico • Singapore • Spain • United Kingdom • United States

Gold Rush

Fast Forward
Green Level 14

Text: Alan Trussell-Cullen
Editor: Johanna Rohan
Design: James Lowe
Series design: James Lowe
Production controller: Emma Hayes
Photo research: Gillian Cardinal
Audio recordings: Juliet Hill, Picture Start
Spoken by: Matthew King and Abbe Holmes
Reprint: Jennifer Foo

Acknowledgements
The author and publisher would like to acknowledge permission to reproduce material from the following sources:
Photographs by Australian Picture Library/Corbis, pp 11, 23/ Bettmann, cover, pp 3, 4, 5 bottom, 13, 16, 22 bottom/ Getty Images, p 9/ Popperfoto, p 8/ E. O. Hoppe, p 20/ Hulton-Deutsch, p 21/ Richard Cummins, p 22 top left; Getty Images/PhotoDisc, p 5 top left/ Hulton Archive, pp 7, 10, 17; National Library of Australia (nla.pic-an10571613-4), p 18; Photolibrary.com/SuperStock/Underwood Photo Archives, back cover, p 5 top right/ Newberry Library, Chicago, p 6/ Claver Carroll, p 15; State Library of Queensland (9190), p 19.

ISBN 978 0 17 012591 8
ISBN 978 0 17 012585 7 (set)

Cengage Learning Australia
Level 7, 80 Dorcas Street
South Melbourne, Victoria Australia 3205
Phone: 1300 790 853

Cengage Learning New Zealand
Unit 4B Rosedale Office Park
331 Rosedale Road, Albany, North Shore NZ 0632
Phone: 0800 449 725

For learning solutions, visit **cengage.com.au**

Printed in Australia by Ligare Pty Ltd
7 8 9 10 11 12 13 21 20 19 18 17

Evaluated in independent research by staff from the Department of Language, Literacy and Arts Education at the University of Melbourne.

Alan Trussell-Cullen

Contents

Chapter 1

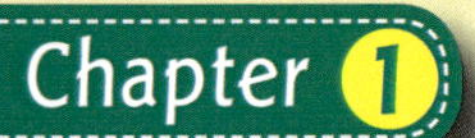

GOLD IN CALIFORNIA

The late 1800s was the time of the great gold rushes.

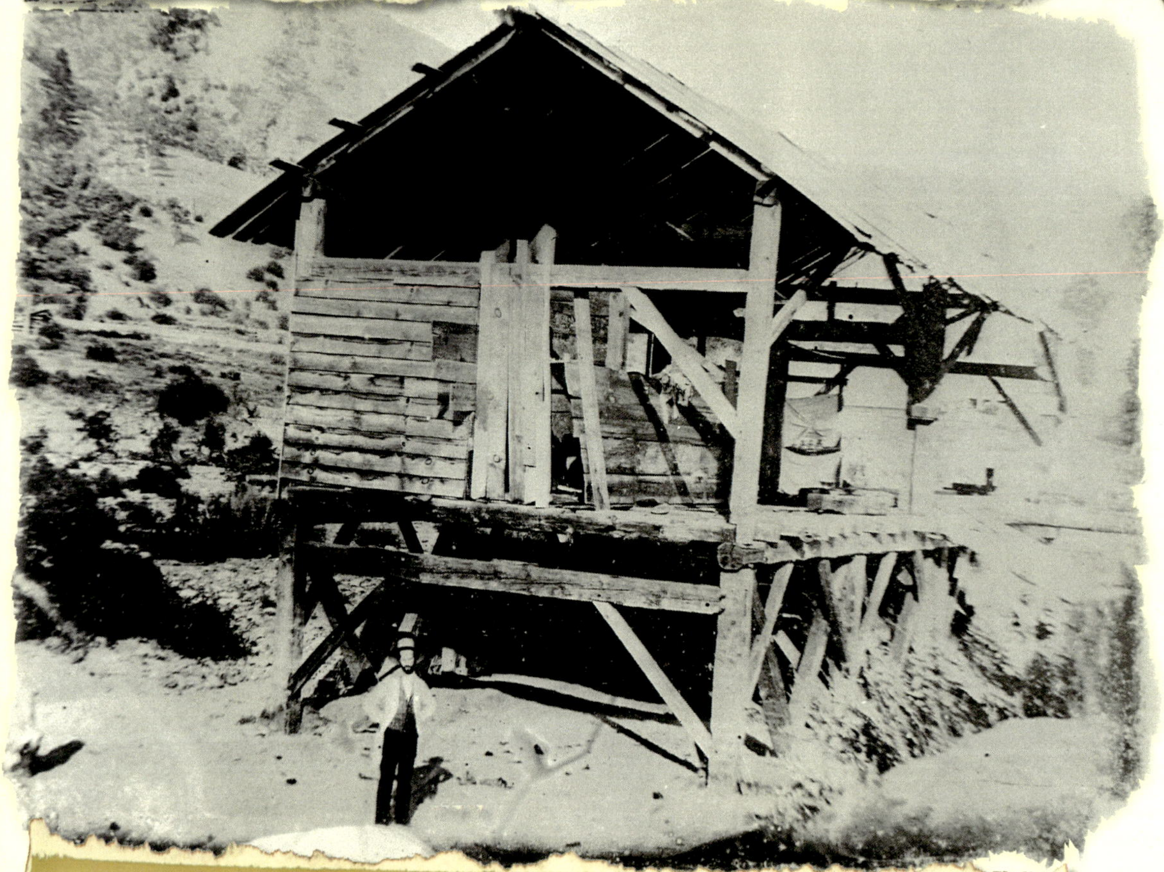

The first big gold rush took place at Sutter's Mill in California. James Marshall, who was working on a farm at Sutter's Mill, found the first bit of gold, in January 1848.

It wasn't long before more gold was found, and the rush began.

Chapter 2

THE RUSH BEGINS

News of the gold travelled fast.
Soon, people from all over America
were heading to California
with the hope of getting rich.

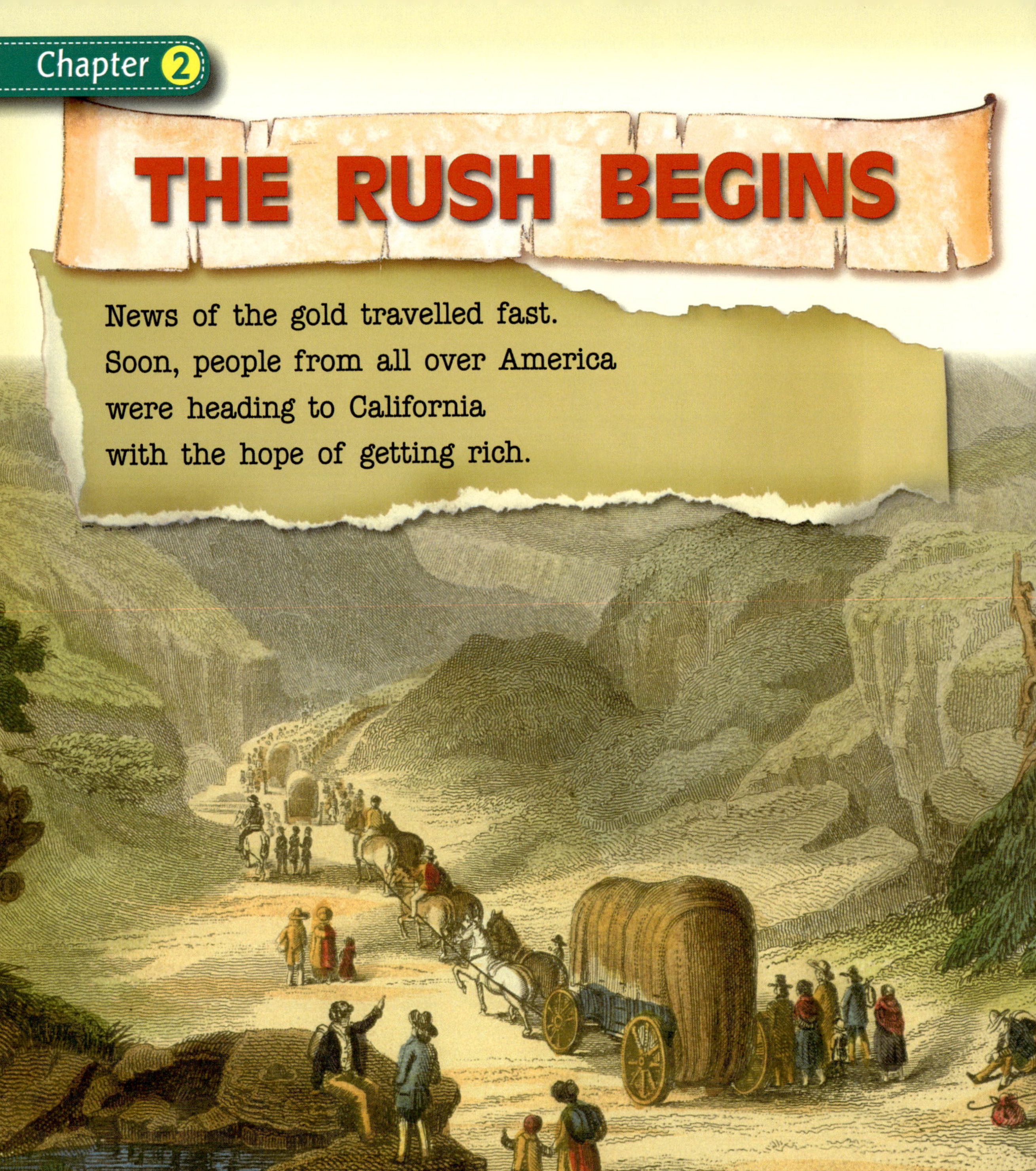

A lot of people travelled across the country.
This was hard to do in those days,
and many people died on the way.

People also came from other countries.
A lot of people came from China.

The people who came to the gold rush in California were called the **forty-niners**.
1849 was the year that most people arrived.

In 1849, the **population** of California jumped from 25000 to 100000 because so many people arrived in California that year.

Life wasn't easy on the goldfields.
Most of the miners lived very close together
in big tent cities.

The food was bad,
and the miners had to pay
a lot of money for it.
People got sick.
There were a lot of fights,
and people were often robbed.

Chapter 3

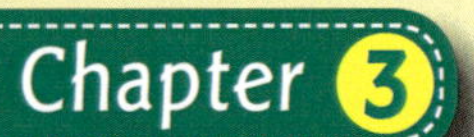

GETTING RICH

Some people found gold and got rich,
but most people didn't.
Many people didn't find any gold at all.

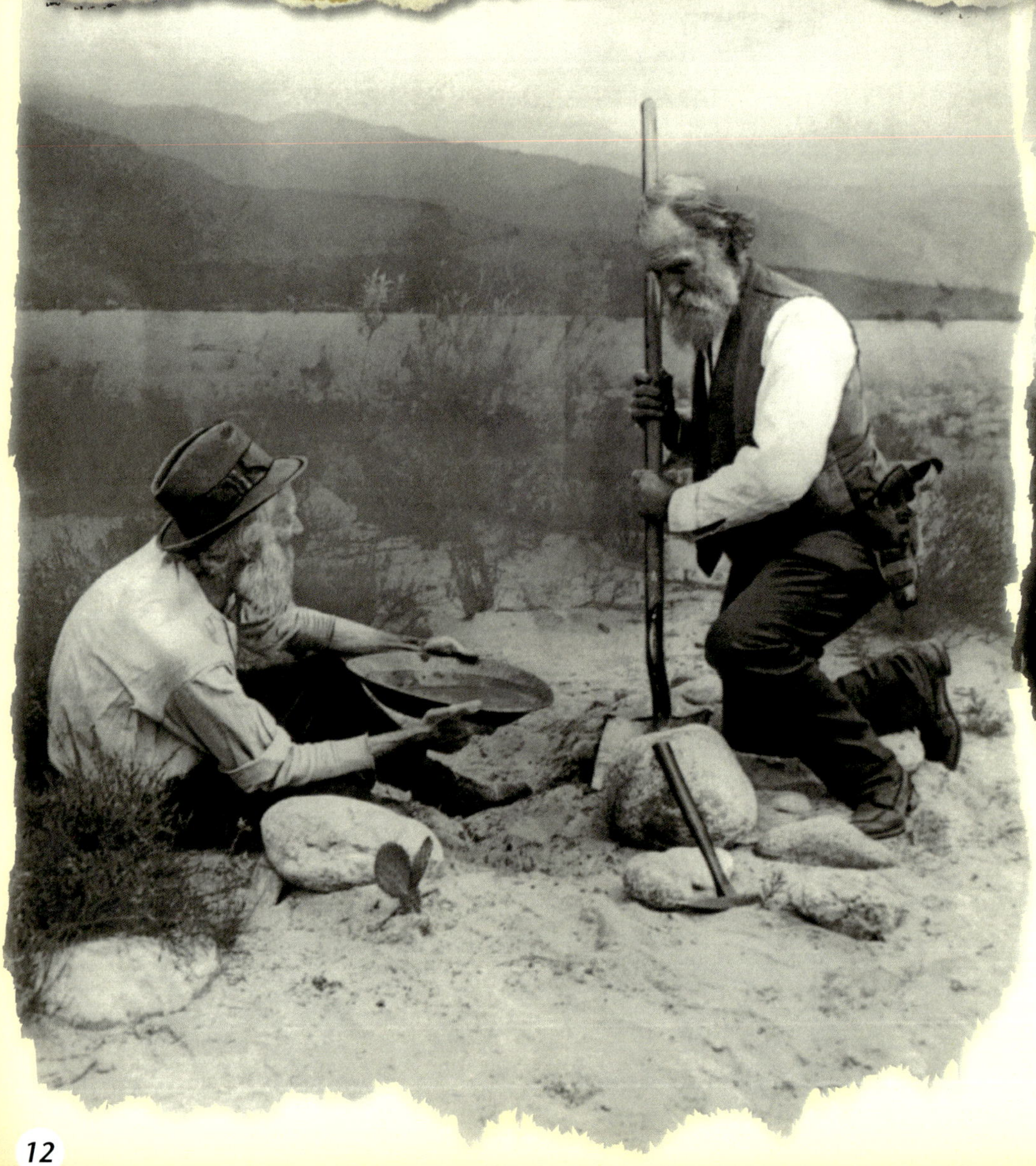

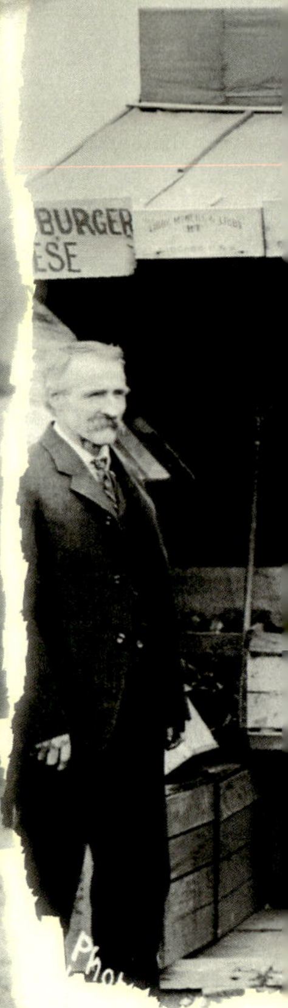

Sometimes, people got rich
by selling food, drink, clothes and pans
to the people looking for gold.

Chapter 4

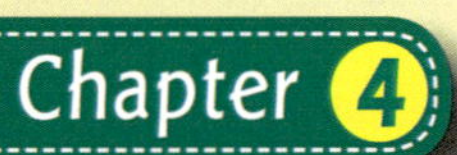

GOLD RUNS OUT

When gold began to run out in California, most people moved on or went home.

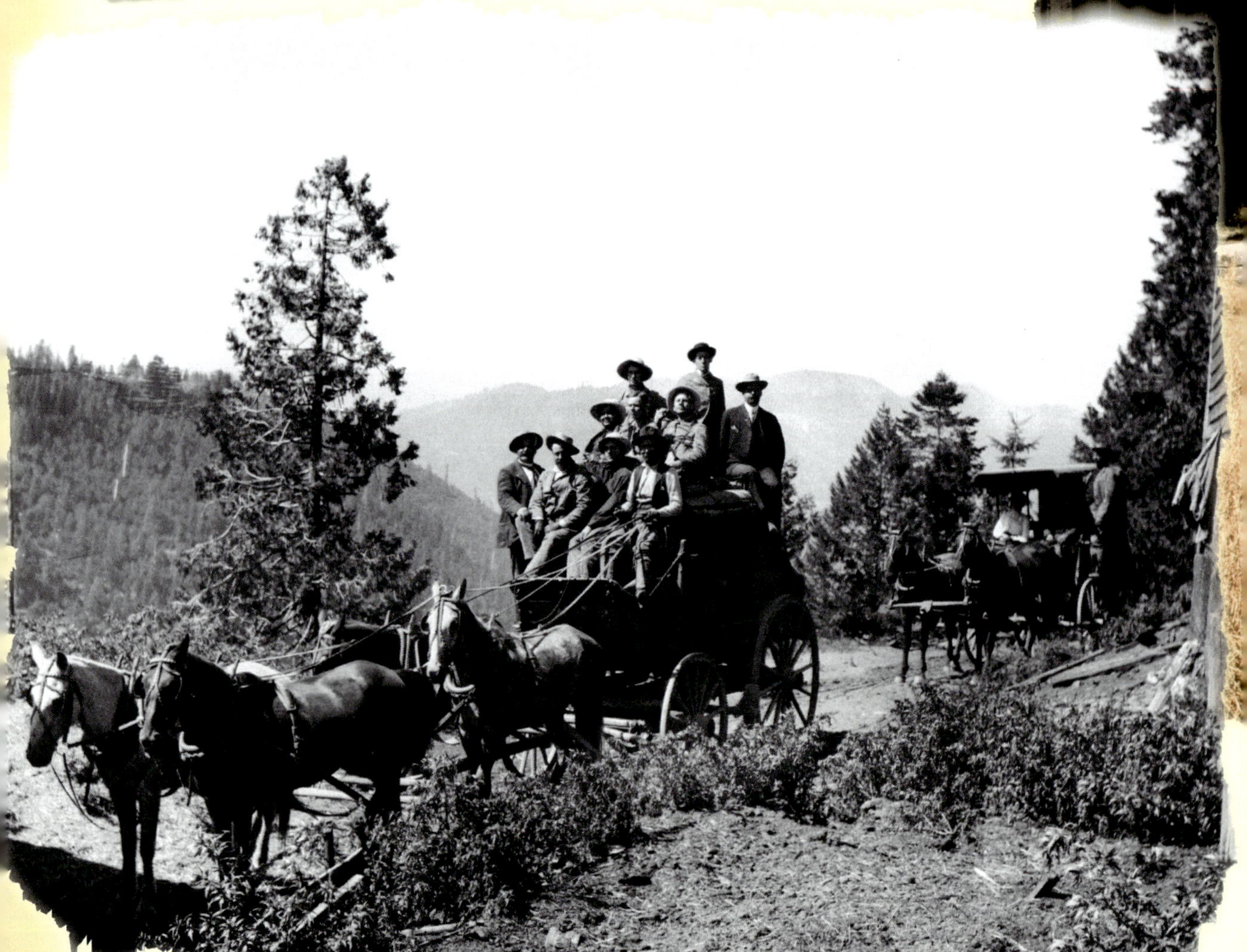

Suddenly, many of the little towns that had popped up near the goldfields became empty.

But, the gold rush also helped to make many places grow bigger.

a gold mining town in Nevada

San Francisco went from being a small town to an important city in just a few years, because of the gold rush.

Chapter 5

GOLD IN AUSTRALIA

When the gold rush in California ended, some of the forty-niners moved to other countries to look for gold.

The next big gold rush was in Australia.
Thousands of people went there hoping to get rich.

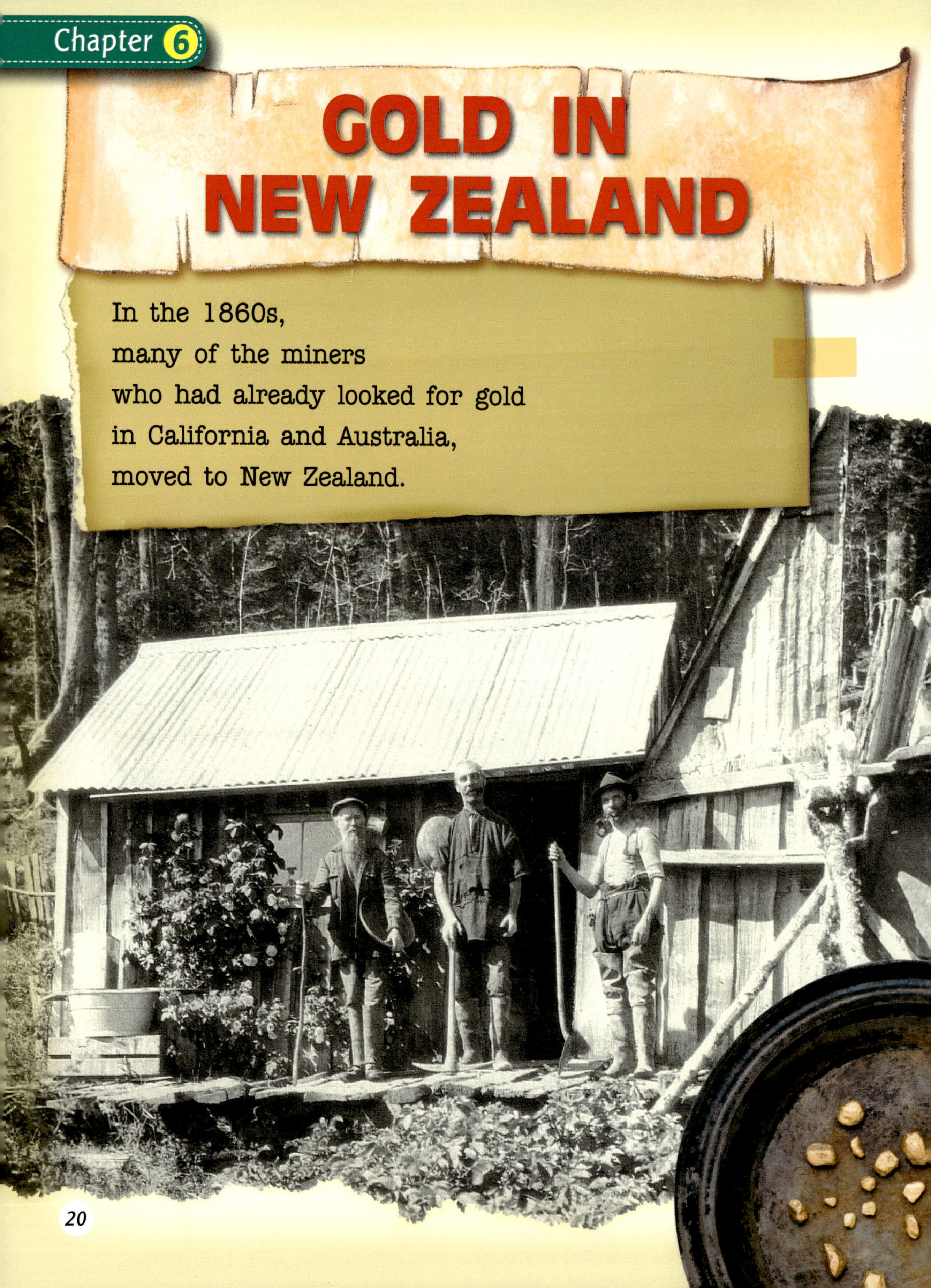

Chapter 6

GOLD IN NEW ZEALAND

In the 1860s,
many of the miners
who had already looked for gold
in California and Australia,
moved to New Zealand.

In 1861, a forty-niner, Gabriel Read,
found gold in New Zealand,
and the gold rush was on.
Over the next six years,
the number of people in New Zealand doubled.

Chapter 7

GOLD IN ALASKA

In 1896, George Carmack found gold in an old creek bed in **the Klondike**, Alaska. He called the creek "Bonanza Creek".

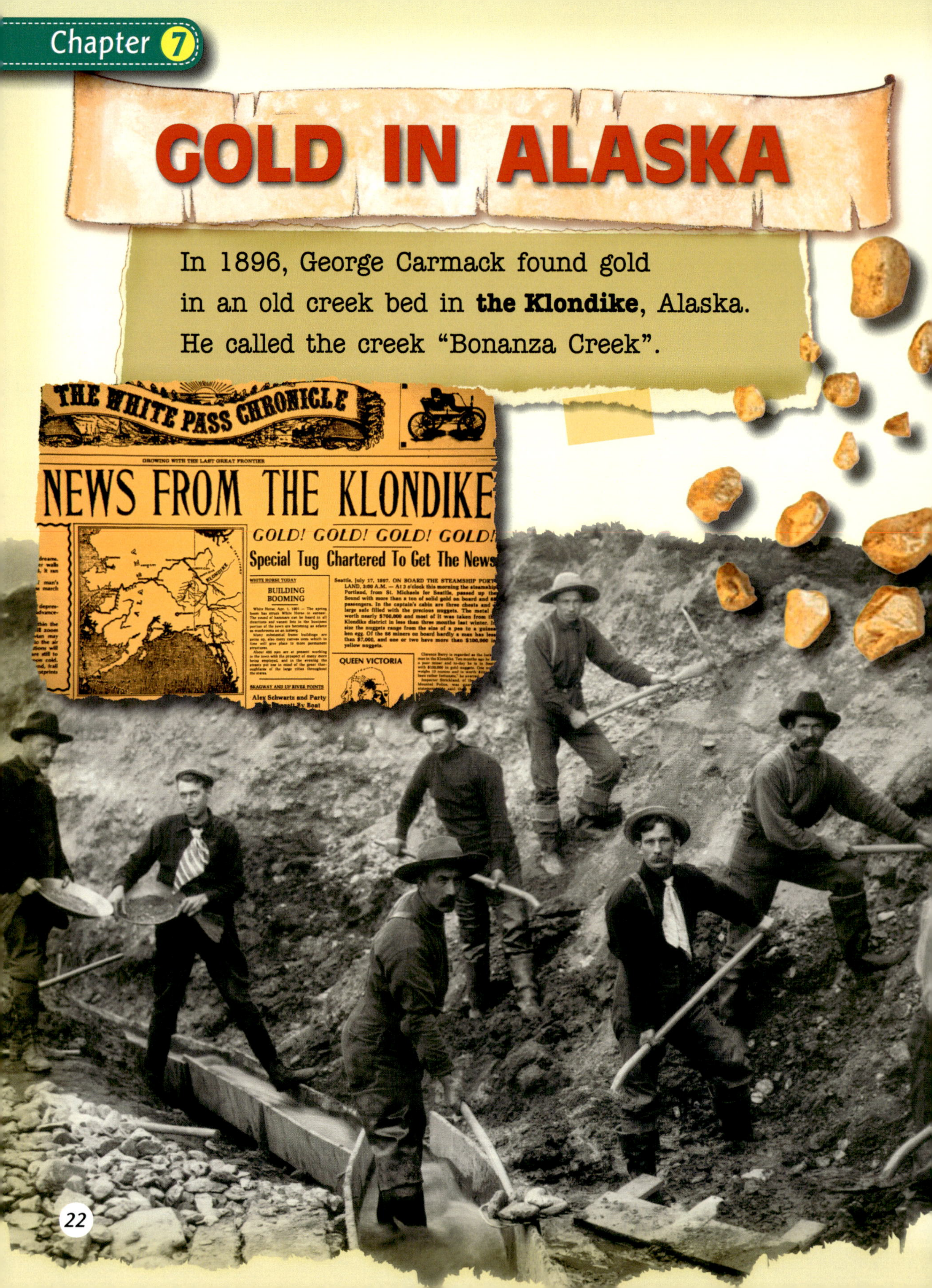

When news of this gold find got out,
thousands of people rushed to the Klondike.
But, because it took so long to get there,
there wasn't much gold left.
The Klondike was the last great gold rush.

Glossary

the Klondike an area in Alaska, in North America

forty-niners gold miners who went to California to find their fortune

population the number of people in one place

Index